For Betty Borell,

with thanks for getting
this playful-foctual book
into the hands of understanding
readers, from her friend,

Richard Cennon

Our
Presidents

OUR
PRESIDENTS

by Richard Armour
Illustrated by Leonard Everett Fisher

Revised and Updated

Woodbridge Press / *Santa Barbara, California*

Published and distributed by

Woodbridge Press Publishing Company
Post Office Box 6189
Santa Barbara, California

Distributed simultaneously in the United States and Canada

Printed in the United States of America

Library of Congress Cataloging in Publication Data

Armour, Richard Willard, 1906–
   Our presidents.

    1. Presidents—United States—Poetry. I. Title.
PS3501.R5508   1983   811'.52   82-23762
ISBN 0-88007-133-8
ISBN 0-88007-134-6 (pbk.)

Acknowledgment

I am grateful to my longtime colleagues, the late Dr. Douglass Adair, Professor of American History, Claremont Graduate School, and Dr. Edward A. White, Nathaniel Wright Stevenson Professor of History and Biography Emeritus, Scripps College, and Professor of History Emeritus, Claremont Graduate School, for their friendly interest and advice. Let me make it clear, however, that neither of these scholarly gentlemen should be held accountable for the result, since I alone am to be blamed for a sometimes irreverent attitude and for an occasional use of poetic license in dealing with the facts and legends of history.

R.A.

Contents

George Washington
1789–1797

When George the Third was
  England's king,
Our George was first in everything:
First in war and peace and hearts—
With him our nation's story starts.

Instead of picking cherries, he
Saved time by chopping down
  the tree,
And having thus avoided bother,
He proudly said, "I did it, father!"
And then (or so says Parson
  Weems,
Who sometimes mixed up facts and
  dreams)
He threw—a shiny silver sliver—
A dollar clear across a river,
Though information still we lack
On whether Georgie got it
  back. . . .

George Washington loved truth
  and justice,
Mount Vernon farm, and Martha
  Custis.
He married Martha, thought to
  spend
His days a farmer, to the end,
But heard the shot heard round
  the world
And round his gun his fingers
  curled,
Then packed his bags, put on
  his hat,
And left his farm, and that was
  that.

At Boston, Trenton, Valley Forge,
The troops were led by George,
  by George,
And "Let George do it," was
  the cry.
George did it, too, none can deny.

He even crossed the Delaware
From shore to shore, from here
  to there,
While standing up (some strong
  men fainted)
So he could have his picture
  painted.
A brilliant leader in the field,
At last he made the British yield,
And helped by Lafayette, from
  France,
Kicked Lord Cornwallis
  in the pants.

Back at his farm, he soon was
  sent for
To be the nation's President, for
He had the kind of kindly look
That looks good in a history book,
The kind of face someday to fill
The bill upon a dollar bill.
He served one term and then a
  second,
But still Mount Vernon always
  beckoned.
"Another term," the people pled,
But no, he quit while still ahead,
And, most retiring man of men,
Went back to farming once again.

John Adams
1797–1801

Many the Adamses, all through our history,
And which one was which is to many a mystery.
We've John and John Quincy and Henry and Samuel,
And some are alike as two humps on a cam-u-el.
But only the Johns have the top office won:
John and John Quincy, father and son.

John Adams was short and short-tempered as well.
When angry he stiffened and clanged like a bell.
He was cross, off and on, a good part of his life,
But rarely with Abigail Adams, his wife.
In spite of his coldness, the glare in his glance,
He kept us at peace with a quarrelsome France
And did what he could, when the times were quite skittish,
At the Court of St. James's, with bull-headed British.

Not first at so much as was Washington, still
This scholar, debater, and man of great skill,
This honest man, earnest man, patriot always,
Who warred with his pen and who argued in hallways,
Was first to be second and serve as Vice-President
And first in the White House to live as a resident
And first among Presidents, border to border,
When listed in alphabetical order.

A

is

for

ADAMS

Thomas Jefferson
1801–1809

In love with column and with dome,
  This most amazing fellow
Designed himself a classic home
  And called it Monticello.

He took the violin in hand
  And really made it squeak.
He studied law and science and
  Read Latin, French, and Greek.

This book collector, educator,
  With talents more to spare,
Invented things like the dumb-waiter
  And (who's dumb?) swivel chair.

He changed the British pounds and pence
  (For this we should be thankful)
To dollars—each a hundred cents—
  And who'd not like a bankful?

He organized the Democrats
  And, just to be amusing,
Called them Republicans, and that's,
  To some, a bit confusing.

He bought Louisiana, he
  Expanded west the nation.
And is this all? Well, now let's see . . .
  He wrote the Declaration.

Tom Jefferson was wise and clever,
  Admired and praised by many.
He thought men equal. He, however,
  Was equaler than any.

James Madison
1809–1817

Though modest, meek,
With frail physique,
No dashing, flashing hero,
James Madison,
When all was done,
Was very far from zero.

For he, you see,
Sought liberty
And found the right solution.
He's known, with love,
As father of
Our rugged Constitution.

And though he let
The British get
Their troops clear into town
And put to torch
And singe and scorch
And burn the White House down,

His good wife Dolley,
Strong and jolly
And unafraid of flames,
Saved precious things—
Like diamond rings
And busts and mugs
And chairs and rugs
And candlesticks
And unburnt bricks
And dresses, hats—and James.

James Monroe
1817–1825

One thing was proved by James Monroe,
  One truth without a catch to it:
If you'd go down in history
Do something—good or bad—and see
  Your name's what they attach to it.

What did he do? He bluntly told
  The European powers:
"Keep off. Keep out." (His words were clear.)
"You play in your own hemisphere
  And we will play in ours."

It's true that he bought Florida
  From Spain, and some exclaim on it.
But what is he remembered for
By everyone, from shore to shore?
  The Doctrine with his name on it.

John Quincy Adams
1825–1829

What in the world could be greater fun
Than being a famous President's son?
Well, John Quincy Adams, besides the fact
That he had the Quincy his father lacked
And maybe a bust of his Dad on his shelf,
Grew up to be President Adams himself.

Short, stout, and bald, with a piping voice,
He hardly seemed like the People's Choice,
In addition to which, a true Adams, he had
The knack of making everyone mad:
Not only his foes, but his friends, no less—
A skill or a talent that few possess.

But he served his country far more than most
In many a governmental post
And, as full of words as a dictionary,
Declaimed so often and well, so very,
Of things that pleased and of things that appalled him,
That "Old Man Eloquent" everyone called him.

Should you still, by chance, be encountering trouble
With John and John Q., seeing Adamses double,
Rejoice that none of his sons (he had three)
Was ever a President, as was he.

Andrew Jackson
1829–1837

Andrew Jackson came out of the West
  With his pistol well oiled and loaded.
A duel he'd fight any day or night
  If by one sneering word he was goaded.

A corncob pipe this frontiersman puffed,
  As did Rachel, his loving wife.
It's said by his foes, who wrinkled their nose,
  He ate peas with his hunting knife.

Though his spelling was poor, and the upper crust
  Was crusty, and snobs were snickery,
The people adored this man with the sword,
  Whom they called, with affection, "Old Hickory."

Ever the fighter, with no holds barred,
  And given to fits of rancor,
The British he slew, and the Seminoles too,
  And he terrified many a banker.

He rescued New Orleans from its siege
  (The pirate, Lafitte, came in handy),
And the masses O.K.'d him and happily made him
  The People's President, Andy.

A red-blooded President, one of the folks,
  Forthright and fearless and hearty,
He spoiled for a fight, and with spoils left and right
  He came to the aid of his Party.

This rough man, this tough man from Tennessee,
  This man who was larger than real,
Was homespun, they say, at home and away,
  And his backbone was spun of steel.

Martin Van Buren
1837–1841

Martin Van Buren,
The Little Magician,
Put the "polite"
Into "politician."

Smiling and courteous,
Kindly of look,
He was known as the Fox
Of Kinderhook.

But all of his charm
Didn't help him much,
And this Dutchman managed
To get in Dutch.

For along came the Panic
Of '37,
And the people begged
And they prayed to Heaven,

And they blamed Van Buren
For all of their woes,
For their empty stomachs
And tattered clothes.

They vented their wrath
As the people can,
Crying, "Van! Van!
Is a used-up man!"

And they turned him out
When next they voted,
And his friends were sad
And his enemies gloated.

William Henry Harrison
1841

Tippecanoe and Tyler too!"
Was the cry that elected Harrison, who
At Tippecanoe the fierce Indians downed
In a battle that won the nation more ground.

At Tippecanoe he had made his name,
Which was legally Harrison, just the same.
But he came to the White House years too late,
The oldest elected, at sixty-eight.

By the time his inaugural speech was spoken
(The longest on record), his health was broken,
And from longest speech, now a man infirm,
It was only a step to the shortest term.

From shaking the hand of every Whig
Who came seeking office (the crowd was big)
And going outdoors with no overcoat on
(Who could tell a President what to don?),

He caught a cold in the chest and head
And after a month in office was dead;
Only thirty days till the poor man cracked:
He was hardly settled and barely unpacked.

The first of our Presidents, he, to die
In the White House, and there in state to lie. . . .
They carried out Harrison, still and thin,
And the door being open, Tyler walked in.

John Tyler
1841–1845

The Whigs said, "Tyler is our man."
  They thought he'd do their bidding.
But Tyler told them, "Think again,"
  And Tyler wasn't kidding.

He vetoed every bill in sight,
  Nor did he once relax.
His sharp quill pen cut left and right
  As if a knife, or ax.

Whigs tried to drive John Tyler out,
  They bullied him and banged him.
Once, with a piece of rope quite stout,
  In effigy they hanged him.

But Tyler went his own sweet way,
  Showed not a bruise or scratch,
And even men like Henry Clay
  Found they had met their match.

Yes, Tyler signed with steady pen.
  His vetoes fell like snow.
And was he re-elected then,
  Or nominated? No.

James K. Polk
1845–1849

James K. Polk
  Said, "Let's annex us
Land from Oregon
  Clear through Texas."

James K. Polk,
  Who wouldn't take "No,"
Out-bargained the British,
  Beat Mexico.

James K. Polk,
  Steady and firm,
Accomplished his aims
  In a single term.

James K. Polk
  Did all he could.
If he wasn't great,
  He was very good.

Yet such is the way
  Of our fickle folk
That few remember
  James K. Polk.

E PLURIBUS UNUM

Zachary Taylor
1849–1850

Zachary Taylor, it ought to be noted,
Never held office, or even voted,
Till he ran for President and, we'd guess,
Cast his very first vote for himself, no less.

As General Taylor, he'd won before.
The hero, he was, of the Mexican War,
Where he battled to triumph with sword and gun
Though outnumbered by Mexicans four to one.

A short, stubby man, he looked taller, of course,
In his General's hat, and astride a horse,
But he had to dismount at the White House door
And then looked as stubby as ever before.

He was tough as leather and brave and steady.
When anyone called him "Old Rough and Ready,"
He bowed politely and doffed his hat.
It was better than "Zachary," maybe, at that.

But rough as he was, he couldn't survive
The day of a President, nine to five.
One Fourth of July he stayed too long
In the broiling sun with a holiday throng,

And he ate fresh cherries and ate and ate,
And he drank iced milk—and it's sad to state:
After sixteen months, a short while indeed,
His term hadn't yet expired, but he'd.

Millard Fillmore
1850–1853

Millard Fillmore broke the rule
That everyone should go to school.

He bought himself some books instead
And read and read and read and read.

This self-made man went up the line:
Vice-President at forty-nine,

Then, helped by Taylor's milk and cherries,
At fifty, President. When Perry's

Ships opened up Japan to see
What was inside, who sent him? He.

Who lent a hand to quench the flame
When Congress' Lib'ry burnt? The same.

And when the Union hit foul weather,
Who tried to hold the states together?

Fillmore again, through compromise
Of every kind and shape and size.

With all he did, or tried to do,
An honest man, and kindly too,

It's really sad that we don't thrill more
To hear the name of Millard Fillmore.

Franklin Pierce
1853–1857

A handsome man was Franklin Pierce,
  And looks are quite a factor.
He might have been a movie star
Had he not studied for the bar,
  Or else an actor.

He had the manner, had the means,
  He also had the knowledge.
His voice rang clearly as a bell;
Longfellow, Hawthorne he knew well
  At Bowdoin College.

He loved a party, any kind,
  On this we're quite emphatic.
But many things he did suggest
The kind of party he loved best
  Was Democratic.

The nation prospered under Pierce,
  It had a sunny season.
The Treasury was crammed with gold
And times were good. But Pierce, we're told,
  Was not the reason.

It's true he maybe signed some bills
  And maybe even banned some.
But when it comes to any quiz,
The most that most remember is
  That he was handsome.

James Buchanan
1857–1861

Buchanan was a bachelor. He led a single life.
A tall, upstanding, wealthy man, why did he get no wife?

Some say he had a sweetheart once who would have been
    his bride,
But they, alas, had quarreled, and the girl soon after died.

This may be true, but those who know Buchanan's record well
Suggest another reason, which they're very glad to tell:

Four years he paced the White House floor, and faced first
    North, then South.
Caught half between a Yes and No, he couldn't move his mouth.

He couldn't lift his pen, or if he lifted it he'd frown
And wonder why he'd lifted it, and slowly set it down.

He wrinkled up his troubled brow, he rubbed his chin and neck.
He was a Chief Executive who never could exec.

He kept from doing wrong, he thought, by simply sitting tight,
But while he kept from doing wrong, he kept from doing right.

And doing neither right nor wrong was wrong, the people said.
The country had a leader but it wasn't being led.

Now is it any wonder one who couldn't make his mind up,
A man as cautious as Old Buck, a bachelor would wind up?

Abraham Lincoln
1861–1865

Abe Lincoln was a tall man,
　A lanky six-feet-four.
He had to duck a little
　When coming through a door,
Yet never was he known to flee
Or duck responsibility.

Abe Lincoln was a strong man,
　A wrestler in his youth.
He wrestled with his conscience,
　He wrestled with the truth,
And won at splitting rails, at fairs,
When other men were splitting hairs.

Abe Lincoln was a man's man,
　Yet women touched his life:
His mother, his stepmother,
　And Mary Todd, his wife.
(His face was lined, in part, by God,
In part, they say, by Mary Todd.)

They called him "Honest Abe"
　And "Father Abraham,"
"The Great Emancipator,"
　"Gorilla," too, and "Sham,"
And whether it was praise or blame
He always took it much the same.

Abe Lincoln's sense of humor
　Was such a saving grace
It turned the dark to brightness,
　Transformed his homely face,
And brought to people, when he spoke,
Large wisdom in a little joke.

Abe Lincoln was a tall man,
　A lanky six-feet-four.
He had to duck a little
　When coming through a door,
And, strangely, everyone he knew
From knowing him, felt taller too.

Andrew Johnson
1865–1869

Andrew Johnson, the Tennessee tailor,
Awaited the word as Lincoln grew paler.
When Lincoln died, Johnson read in his will:
"Here are my shoes, they are yours to fill."

Poor Andy, inheriting riot and ruction,
Was faced with the problems of reconstruction.
The Civil War was over and won,
But his war with Congress was barely begun.

A hot-tempered fellow and stubborn was he.
The slaves had been freed, and no slave he'd be.
The reason his struggle with Congress was grim
Was that Congress, in turn, wouldn't bow to him.

Many a slanderous slogan was coined,
And gavels were banged, as the battle was joined.
Vetoes and votes clashed like swords in the night
As Johnson and Congress fought their fight.

It was nip and tuck, it was tup and nick.
If Congress was nimble, Johnson was quick.
Each had a grip on the other's throat,
And Johnson was saved by A SINGLE VOTE.

Only one more vote would have played real hob
And have cost Old Andy his White House job.
Republican, Whig, or Democrat,
No President's ever come closer than that!

Ulysses S. Grant
1869–1877

General Grant was as hard as granite,
  Defeating General Lee.
He puffed a cigar
While he won the war.
  As hard as a stone was he.

But President Grant was as soft as syrup
  When leading a strife-torn land.
The way he would bend
Just to please a friend
  Proved him soft as a baby's hand.

Rumor has it that in Grant's Tomb,
  A tomb that is tall and wide,
General Grant
And President Grant
  Lie peacefully side by side.

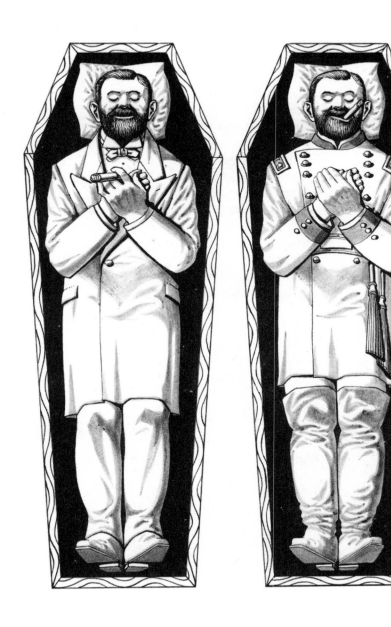

Rutherford B. Hayes
1877–1881

A stalwart reformer
   Was Rutherford Hayes,
Determined to straighten
   Men's devious ways.

His lips touched no liquor,
   Strong drink he rejected.
His beard was so bushy
   His lips were protected.

His wife, too, drank water
   And punches fruit-juicy,
Which won her the nickname
   Of Lemonade Lucy.

Though barely elected
   (Some questioned the ballot),
Once in, he struck spoilsmen
   As if with a mallet.

Sound money he wanted,
   Sound government, too,
And the sound that he heard
   From opponents was "Boo!"

Oh, Rutherford Hayes
   Was a bearded crusader,
A hard-money man,
   Soft-drink lemonader.

He went to bed early
   And early he riz,
And he knew of two viewpoints:
   The wrong one and his.

James A. Garfield
1881

Poor Garfield, oh, poor Garfield,
  The most beset of men!
For one whom he appointed
  He disappointed ten.
For one whom he made happy
  Ten others he enraged.
Each month he stayed in office
  Two years poor Garfield aged.

Four months had passed, when, *horrors!*
  A disappointed hack
Stepped up quite close to Garfield
  And shot him in the back.
Long weeks poor Garfield lingered
  Upon his bed of pain,
But though the doctors doctored,
  Their efforts were in vain.

So Garfield died a martyr,
  By death made almost holy.
Eleven weeks he suffered,
  He died so very slowly,
Whereas the man whose bullet
  Gave him the fatal banging
Was relatively lucky—
  His death came fast, from hanging.

Chester A. Arthur
1881–1885

The shot that killed Garfield shot Arthur from Vice
Up to President, which (for Prince Arthur) was nice.
His friends never dreamt that he ever would get
To such a high place, not (good gracious, no) Chet!

For Chester A. Arthur, side whiskers and all,
Was a dude and a dandy, good-looking and tall.
His cellar was stocked with the finest of wines
Or, his tongue slightly twisted, "the winest of fines."

And his wardrobe? This elegant man of affairs
Is famed for his trousers—he had eighty pairs!
And the crease upon each was as sharp, people say,
As a blade, and a blade (gay) was Chester A. A.

But the greatest surprise to his friends, the sensation,
Wasn't Chester's becoming the head of the nation.
What came as a shock was that Chester the Charmer,
The slightly spoiled spoilsman, became a reformer!

And to friends who'd expected their share of the loot
When Garfield was shot in the rear of his suit,
To friends who'd been patiently waiting and trusting,
This change in old Chet was, well, downright disgusting.

Grover Cleveland
1885–1889

Grover the Good was built like a boulder,
  As solid as rock was he.
He was thick in the chest and wide in the shoulder,
  And his chin was as firm as could be.

Grover was honest and Grover was just,
  As just as a justice he was.
Calling "public office a public trust,"
  He set politicians a-buzz.

Grover was first in the White House to marry
  And bring there a bride brand-new.
He was then forty-nine (he was one to tarry),
  While his wife was but twenty-two.

Grover tried hard, oh so hard, to do right.
  He was always unbendingly serious.
Four years of such goodness, however, just might
  Be inclined, since we're human, to weary us,

As it must have the voters in Grover's day,
  Because, as you may have suspected,
Despite all the good Grover did, we must say,
  With regret, he was not re-elected.*

*Until later. See page 56.

Benjamin Harrison
1889–1893

Benjamin Harrison barely got in.
His margin of votes was thinner than thin.
In fact, as we've learned on the best of authority,
He won by a hundred thousand *minority!*

What helped Ben get in was the fact that he had
A President grandfather, Congressman Dad,
And his great-grandfather had been a signer
Of the Declaration. What could be finer?

Now Ben himself, who was long on family,
Was short on height, and he shook hands clammily.
Standing five-feet-six, he mounted when able
A step or a platform or even a table.

A Sunday school teacher, reserved and quiet,
Little Ben wasn't what you would call a riot,
No life of the Party, no jolly good scout,
As fellow Republicans soon found out.

With his clammy handshake and eyes of steel,
Ben somehow was lacking in Prex appeal,
And though he did nothing terribly wrong,
The four years he served seemed twice that long.

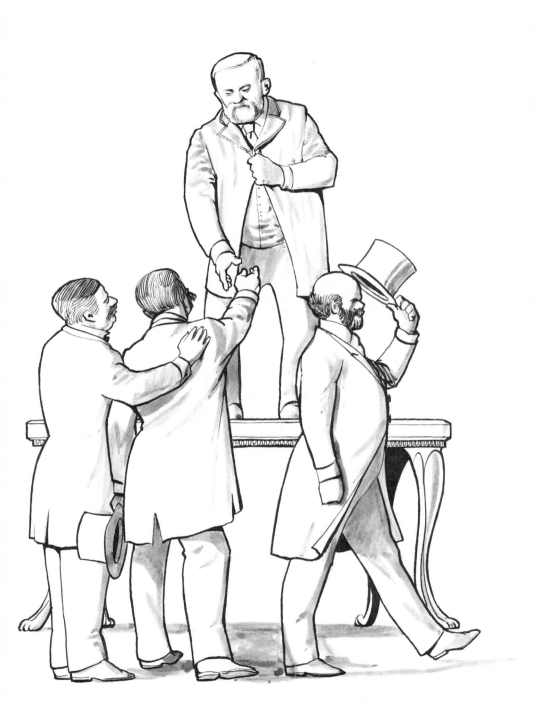

Grover Cleveland
1893–1897

After comparison
With Benjamin Harrison
It was good to have Grover
Cleveland all over.

William McKinley
1897–1901

Anti-hard times
And pro-prosperity,
McKinley believed
In love and charity.

He loved Big Business
And little brown brotherhood;
He hissed at sin
And applauded motherhood.

He trusted in God
And he trusted in trusts
And the full dinner pail
(And not filled with crusts).

Many a hand
He shook, around town,
But the hand didn't shake
That shot him down.

With his heart of gold
And his spirit true blue,
McKinley went straight—
But the bullet did too.

Oh, McKinley was loved
From Platte to Peoria,
And he died the same year
As Queen Victoria.

Theodore Roosevelt
1901–1909

By Godfrey!" cried Teddy, and "Bully!" he cried,
  "Why, war isn't frightful, it's fun."
And he opened his mouth
To the north and the south
  And his teeth shone right back at the sun.

A red-blooded blue-blood, he built himself up
  With dumbbells and boxing until,
Shooting Spaniards remorseless,
He galloped, though horseless,
  Shouting, "Charge, men!" up San Juan Hill.

Oh yes, he ran up, but he never ran down,
  His energy being quite boundless.
"Speak softly," he said,
But from all we have read,
  He himself only rarely was soundless.

He fought and he ranched and he wrote and he rode,
  And he never sat still for a minute.
When they said the Canal
Couldn't be, he said, "Pal,
  Here's a shovel, go on and begin it."

He made the dirt fly, and the fur fly, too,
  Sent the Navy around-the-world cruising,
And with a Big Stick
With which he was quick
  Busted trusts and big game, never losing.

In his steel-circled spectacles, "Teddy," "T. R.,"
  (Or "Four-Eyes," some said on the side),
Was himself quite a spectacle,
Wild and imprectacle,
  And a boy till the day he died.

William Howard Taft
1909–1913

A chair of special size it took
  For William Howard Taft,
And how the walls and windows shook
  When William Howard laughed.

At Yale a scholar—athlete, too—
  He was Old Eli's pride,
Though if he stood quite high, it's true
  He also stood quite wide.

The Philippines he kept in trim,
  He smoothed out every kink,
Despite the fear that under him
  The islands all might sink.

The White House, built for smaller men,
  He found a constant rub.
They called the plumber now and then
  To pry him from the tub.

And after eating, when he drowsed
  At some affair of state,
He more than once was rudely roused—
  The chair crashed from his weight.

Supreme Court? He did better there.
  No need to pry or wrench.
Instead of on a fragile chair,
  He sat upon the bench.

Thus the career of Taft you see,
  Three-hundred-fifty pounder.
Some Presidents were square as he,
  No President was rounder.

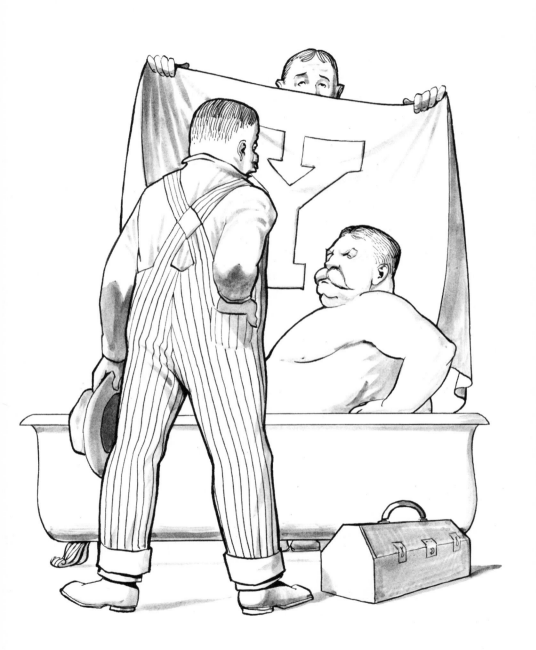

Woodrow Wilson
1913–1921

When Woodrow Wilson set his jaw,
Some looked with fear, some looked with awe,
For it was quite a jaw to set,
A sight you wouldn't soon forget.
His spine, too, was unbending, stiff.
He was as cozy as a cliff.
Yet if not human, he inclined
To kindliness toward humankind.

Aristocratic democrat,
He often wore a tall silk hat
Upon his head, while in his head
Were books he'd written, books he'd read,
Containing vision, hope, and plan
Whereby to help the little man
Who had no shiny topper tall,
In fact who had no hat at all.

Head in the clouds, he'd sometimes go
A route that baffled men below:
He hated war, hoped wars would cease,
Yet fought a war to keep the peace,
Then having fought, at mortal cost,
Thought he had won when he had lost.
He first taught history, then wrought
More history than he had taught.

Schoolmaster President, his school
Was all the world, and with his rule
He rapped the knuckles of the Kaiser
And left him somewhat sadder, wiser.
But he himself, from things unplanned on,
Was left without a League to stand on,
And, stiffly stubborn to the end,
He broke because he wouldn't bend.

Warren Gamaliel Harding
1921–1923

Handsome Harding, with outstretched hand,
  Possessor of well-pressed pants—
He blew a horn in his home town band,
  But later he blew his chance.

They picked him out in a smoke-filled room
  Where no one could see too well.
And first they exulted, and then there was gloom,
  When thanks to friend Fall, he fell.

Back-slapping Harding, the bosses' choice,
  Plagued rather by friend than by foe.
As loud as the horn he once blew was his voice,
  But he choked when he tried to say "No."

His White house job gave him little joy,
  Though poker with cronies he played there.
Alas, poor Harding, the small-town boy,
  Who'd been happier had he stayed there.

Calvin Coolidge
1923–1929

Calvin Coolidge pinched a penny,
   He also pinched a nickel.
He looked a little pinched himself,
As if he had, a lean-faced elf,
   Been weaned upon a pickle.

An honest, cautious, modest man,
   Of long Vermonter line,
He took his exercise, perforce,
Indoors, on an electric horse,
   And got to bed by nine.

And while some railed at Prohibition,
   Thought it a dirty trick,
It didn't bother Calvin much,
For just a teeny little touch
   Of liquor made him sick.

No orator was Silent Cal,
   For talking never noted.
And since, when something must be said,
He'd simply nod or shake his head,
   He rarely was misquoted.

He held his tongue (with both his hands)
   Until his term was done.
One time he let it go, one breach,
Was when he made his famous speech:
   "I do not choose to run."*

*And he didn't.

Herbert Hoover
1929–1933

Hoover's career as an engineer
We should, at the outset, explain.
For he was the kind who mapped and who mined,
Not the kind who could pilot a train.

With shovel and pick did he burrow and nick,
And long was his working day.
Then when he struck gold and grew rich, we are told
Large amounts this good man gave away.

For Hoover, it's plain, was extremely humane.
Feeding Belgians became his great cause.
In his stiffly starched collar this chubby-faced scholar
Was a sort of a Santa Claus.

So he was elected, and as was expected
Soon had things in streamlined condition.
(One streamlining scheme was his lining a stream,
For whenever he could, he went fishin'.)

Then came, though, hard times, turning dollars to dimes,
And people each day grew forlorner.
But Herb cried, "Hurrah!" insisting he saw
Prosperity just round the corner.

When the stock market crashed, Hoover still unabashed
The signs of disaster ignored.
He held his chin high. And can you guess why?
With that collar, it couldn't be lowered.

Franklin Delano Roosevelt
1933–1945

Franklin D. Roosevelt, "F. D. R.,"
Led us in peace and led us in war,
Led us by night and led us by day,
And everyone hoped that he knew the way.

Squire of Hyde Park, fifth cousin of Teddy,
He smiled and he waved at each Tom, Dick, and Eddie.
He turned on the charm, as a Roosevelt can,
And he never forgot the Forgotten Man.
"My friends," he began, in his Fireside Chats,
And his words were like hundreds of Welcome mats,
And each of his listeners, gay or grim,
Thought F. D. R. was talking to *him*.

Though multitudes loved him, many men hated him,
And "Traitor!" "That Man in the White House!" berated him.
They deeply distrusted his Brain Trust's brains,
And packing the Court gave them shooting pains.
They suddenly suffered a sickening feeling
Whenever they thought of his newest New Dealing
And breaking tradition as four-time President
And maybe becoming a permanent resident.

But he picked up the ball where Herb Hoover had dropped it,
He slowed the Depression and finally stopped it,
He Commander-in-Chiefed till we won over Hitler
And the Japanese warlords felt littler and littler,
He kept us abreast and ahead of the times,
He started the march of the March of Dimes,
He named the Four Freedoms and brought them to life,
He travelled the world (and so did his wife).

Thus F. D. R., with the courage of ten,
Went his merry way as a leader of men.
His cigarette holder, regardless of wrangle,
He jauntily tilted at just the right angle,
And even Republicans had to confess,
"There was something special about him, I guess."

Harry S Truman*
1945–1953

Harry inherited F. D. R.'s shoes,
   And their largeness he quickly detected.
But here is some rather remarkable news:
   He filled them far more than expected.

But F. D. R.'s cigarette holder and cape
   He wisely let stay on the shelf.
For Harry was not one to copy or ape,
   Content to be simply himself.

And being himself meant he played the piano
   And said what he thought with great gusto.
When Margaret sang (operatic soprano),
   Too critical critics he'd bust-o.

No Washington, Wilson, or Jefferson—still
   He had honesty, sureness, acumen,
He did what he did with a resolute will,
   And he always was Harry S Truman.

*There is no period after the "S" in Harry S Truman's name. The "S" is not an
abbreviation of any name, and is said to have been chosen by his parents to
avoid any display of favoritism, since his paternal grandfather's name was
Shippe (Anderson Shippe Truman) and his maternal grandfather's name was
Solomon Young.

Dwight D. Eisenhower
1953–1961

The British never called a king,
Right to his face, some chummy thing.
When Henry VIII was in his carriage,
Returning from another marriage,
Imagine folk of lowest rank
All yelling at him, "Hi, there, Hank!"

But here, democracy in flower,
Who'd bother saying Eisenhower?
Five stars, Supreme Allied Commander,
The President—and yet, with candor,
We must admit we called him Ike,
A name, in fact, he seemed to like.

From cars and planes and steps and platforms
Ike smiled and waved at thin and fat forms,
And "We like Ike!" on every side,
Charmed by his charm, the people cried.
He seemed just like an older brother,
Or father, though they had another.

Though Democrats might sometimes mutter,
"He's less a President than putter,"
Let Ike but grin that boyish grin
And those at outs with him were in.
Throughout the land, from peak to pike,
No one could really dislike Ike.

John F. Kennedy
1961–1963

J FK at 43,
Youngest ever elected, he,
PT boat hero and Harvard man,
One of the numerous Kennedy clan.

Than most of the Presidents, Jack was richer,
A better footballer, better pitcher,
Fuller of vigah, fuller of life,
And he had, without doubt, the loveliest wife.

He wore no hat, but he warmed his head
On the coldest days with his hair instead,
And men who were balding and wore a hat
Sighed, "Oh for a head of hair like that!"

Jack was nimble and Jack was quick,
And his Irish wit warmed his rhetoric.
His youth and his charm caused the crowds to cheer
As he marched up in front of the New Frontier.

A man of courage, a man in his prime,
There was much to do, but he had much time.
He loved his family, loved his nation,
And gave of himself without hesitation.

Yes, life was a challenge, a hard-fought sport,
But life can be long or life can be short.
Not quite three years of his term were done
When a lurking assassin leveled his gun,

And the bullets flew forth from where he hid,
And Kennedy died as Lincoln did.

Lyndon B. Johnson
1963–1969

Lyndon B. Johnson, better known
As LBJ, ascended the throne
(No, it wasn't a throne but it seemed that way)
When that sudden end came to JFK.
A shrewd, strong man, this man of the hour
Loved his country much, but he also loved power,
And he dreamed, though the times were becoming rioty,
Of something described as the Great Society.

LBJ was rough-hewn and tall
And being a Texan he spoke with a drawl.
Thus when he said "Texas," some trembled with fear,
For it sounded like "taxes" to many an ear.
A little like Jackson he was, in a word,
Though his wife wasn't Rachel but Lady Bird.

Many things he did caused both laughter and tears,
Such as hoisting a hound dog up by its ears
And lifting his shirt to show people his scar—
But he couldn't quite win or quite lose a war.
As the light at the end of the tunnel grew dimmer,
His chances of reelection grew slimmer.
So he thought it better to ride than run,
And went back to his horse in the Texas sun.

Richard M. Nixon
1969–1974

Defeated twice, most thought him through,
  Then when he was elected
He felt at last he'd got his due.
  (Some said, "He's resurrected.")

The first election was a squeak,
  A landslide next, instead.
And few could guess, their guessing weak,
  The slide that lay ahead.

For Richard Nixon stopped a war
  That many thought immoral
And brought our boys home from afar—
  A fact with which few quarrel.

To Russia, China, everywhere
  He went to patch up peace,
And words of praise were in the air,
  But these were soon to cease.

For then came Watergate and tapes
  And cover-ups and all,
Impeachment threats in frightful shapes
  And finally the Fall.

Was Nixon good or bad? That we
  To history assign.
He *did* achieve a first, you see:
  First ever to resign.

Gerald R. Ford
1974–1977

Gerald Ford was also first,
First not to be elected,
And Nixon, who appointed him
His Veep, and thus anointed him,
Was pardoned, as expected.

An honest, forthright man was Ford,
A former football player.
Although at times he tumbled
(His toe or tongue he'd fumbled),
He was no weak O.K.er.

For though he had a honeymoon
With Congress, it soon ended.
Its bills he thought outlandish
He vetoed out-of-handish
Unless they were amended.

No charismatic Kennedy,
No F.D.R. all heeded,
At least like Truman
Ford was human,
Though some thought more was needed.

Jimmy Carter
1977–1981

Though Jimmy Carter's name was James
On Jimmy he insisted.
A simple Georgia boy he was,
And sympathy enlisted.

Imagine Tommy Jefferson
Or Johnny Adams, please,
Or Woody Wilson, Billy Taft—
It's hard to think of these.

But Jimmy Carter somehow fits
This man who would be trusted.
Although a reborn Christian, he
Confessed he sometimes lusted.

Rosalynn, his wife, as well
As Amy, his small daughter,
Both served him well, but brother Billy
Raised thoughts, no doubt, of slaughter.

Yes, Carter was a kindly man
Who hoped for human rights.
Equality and peace he sought,
And high he set his sights.

Camp David saw his finest try
For peace, a true disarmer.
But somehow he, as President,
Still seemed a peanut farmer.

Ronald Reagan
1981–

Many films have depicted the notable residents
Of the White House, those powerful leaders, our
    Presidents.
But not until Reagan did Hollywood lend
The White House an actor. (Thus starting a trend?)

Though oldest of Presidents ever elected,
Reagan didn't look nearly as old as expected.
There were lines in his face, but his hair showed no gray,
And he got off his quips in professional way.
Tough from riding the range and from chopping up wood,
A would-be assassin's bold shot he withstood.

Whether his fault or Carter's, alas, our great nation
Was gripped by recession combined with inflation,
And this was the reason a record was set:
A trillion was reached by the national debt!
Unfinished.

Unfinished.

88